OCS Study
MMS 2003-072

Selected Aspects of the Ecology of the Continental Slope Fauna of the Gulf of Mexico: A Synopsis of the Northern Gulf of Mexico Continental Slope Study, 1983-1988

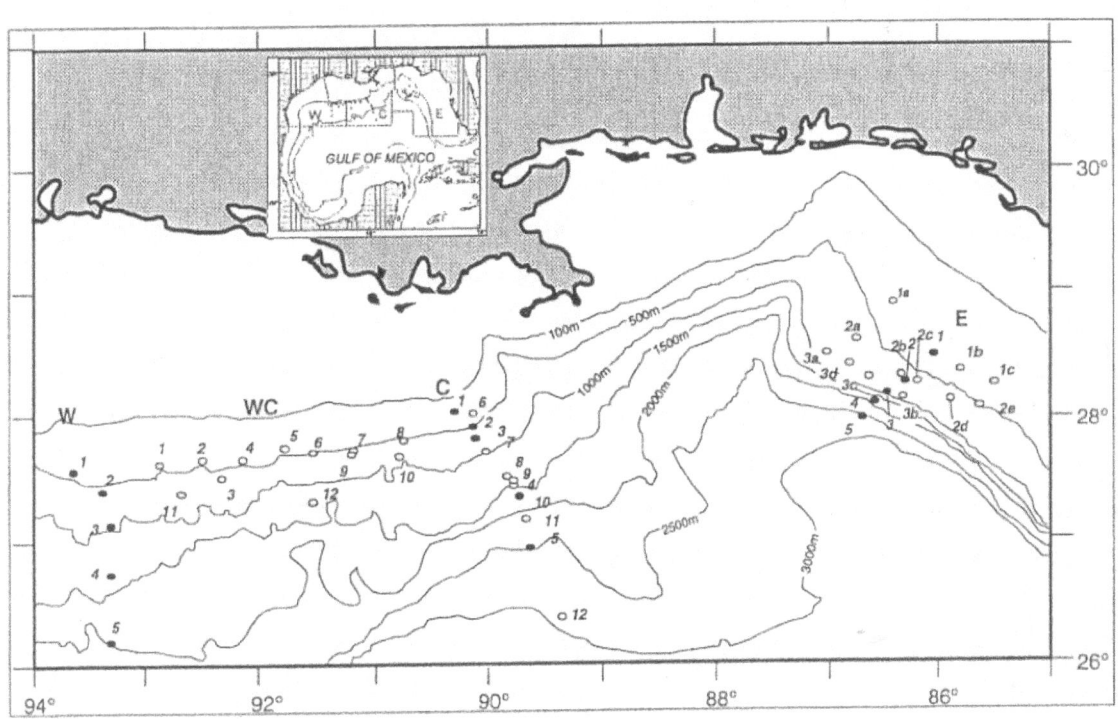

U.S. Department of the Interior
Minerals Management Service
Gulf of Mexico OCS Region

OC3 3ludy
MMS 2003-072

Selected Aspects of the Ecology of the Continental Slope Fauna of the Gulf of Mexico: A Synopsis of the Northern Gulf of Mexico Continental Slope Study, 1983-1988

Authors

Benny J. Gallaway
John G. Cole
Robert G. Fechhelm

Prepared under MMS Purchase Order 17037
by
LGL Ecological Research Associates, Inc.
1410 Cavitt Street
Bryan, Texas 77801

Published by

U.S. Department of the Interior
Minerals Management Service
Gulf of Mexico OCS Region

New Orleans
November 2003

DISCLAIMER

This report was prepared under a purchase order from the Minerals Management Service (MMS) to LGL Ecological Research Associates, Inc. This report has been technically reviewed by the MMS and approved for publication. Approval does not signify that contents necessarily reflect the views and policies of the Service, nor does mention of trade names or commercial products constitute endorsement or recommendation for use. It is, however, exempt from review and compliance with MMS editorial standards.

REPORT AVAILABILITY

Extra copies of this report may be obtained from the Public Information Office (Mail Stop 5034) at the following address:

U.S. Department of the Interior
Minerals Management Service
Gulf of Mexico OCS Region
Public Information Office (MS 5034)
1201 Elmwood Park Boulevard
New Orleans, Louisiana 70123-2394
Telephone: (504) 736-2519 or
1-800-200-GULF

CITATION

Suggested citation:

Gallaway, B.J., J.G. Cole, and R.G. Fechhelm. 2003. Selected aspects of the ecology of the continental slope fauna of the Gulf of Mexico: A synopsis of the Northern Gulf of Mexico Continental Slope Study, 1983-1988. U.S. Department of the Interior, Minerals Management Service, Gulf of Mexico OCS Region, New Orleans, LA. OCS Study MMS 2003-072. 44 pp.

TABLE OF CONTENTS

LIST OF FIGURES

LIST OF TABLES

ABSTRACT

The Minerals Management Service (MMS) funded a Northern Gulf of Mexico Continental Slope (NGOMCS) study which was conducted over the period 1983-1998. The studies were completed and a review of selected aspects were published in the peer-reviewed literature (Pequegnat et al. 1990). A new continental slope study was funded by MMS in the late 1990's. It was subsequently learned that large portions of the historical database had been lost or corrupted. In this study, we have 1) reconstructed and updated the database to include corrections to the data that were made after the contract was completed; 2) conducted new analyses to test the zonation hypothesis proposed in the original study; and 3) prepared a summary of the overall findings. We conclude that the Gulf continental slope appears to differ from the slope fauna of the U.S. Atlantic region in several fundamental ways and that the general pattern of faunal change on the upper slope is that of a non-repeating sequence of species arrayed along the depth gradient rather than three distinct and homogeneous megafaunal assemblages.

INTRODUCTION

By the late 1970s, the continental shelf of the northwestern Gulf of Mexico had become the most intensely developed offshore oil and gas region in the world. Further, new technology was envisioned that would allow movement of oil and gas exploration off the shelf down the continental slope (200-3,000 m in depth). Given this potential expansion of development, the federal agency responsible for regulating offshore oil and gas development (U.S. Department of Interior's Minerals Management Service, MMS) commissioned a synthesis of available environmental and biological information about the continental slope region of the Gulf of Mexico. The results of that study (Pequegnat 1983) characterized the continental slope of the northern Gulf as having five distinctive faunal zones, arranged in broad, depth-delimited bands around the perimeter of the slope. The fauna was generally considered, however, to be poorly known and new studies were proposed as being necessary to evaluate the impacts of oil and gas development in this region.

In response to this recommendation, MMS funded the Northern Gulf of Mexico Continental Slope (NGOMCS) Study which was conducted over the period 1983 to 1988 (Gallaway et al. 1988a; Gallaway 1988a, 1988b, 1988c). The focus of the study centered on testing the hypothesized depth-biological zonation concept, i.e., sampling stations were not evenly spaced down the slope, but were the approximate mid-point of the previously defined biological zones or faunal assemblages. Biota were sampled using box cores (meiofauna, macrofauna), trawls (megafauna), and a benthic camera system (megafauna). Abundance was compared among geographic regions, seasons, and along isobaths as well as by depth. The relationships of faunal abundance to sediment type, sediment and water quality, and hydrocarbon content and type of hydrocarbon were also evaluated. While the study design supported the use of only four basic ANOVA's, there were many species and physical variables to be evaluated. The basic macrofauna correlation matrix was 83 x 83 variables yielding nearly 7,000 correlations. Analysis of the 61 species of abundant macrofauna yielded 244 ANOVA analyses, each with a corresponding set of orthogonal contrasts addressing questions of interest. The findings were presented and discussed in some 2,000 plus pages of the final reports produced for MMS in 1988 as cited above. These gray-literature reports were not widely circulated.

The specimens of meiofauna, macrofauna, and megafaunal invertebrates collected by the NGOMCS Study were transported to the U.S. Museum of Natural History for archival, whereas the fish were deposited at the Texas Cooperative Wildlife Collection, Texas A&M University. Some 48,000 benthic photographs taken during the study were submitted to MMS at the Gulf of Mexico Regional Office in New Orleans, Louisiana. The verified data files collected by the NGOMCS Study were submitted to the National Oceans Data Center (NODC) for archival.

A review of the selected aspects of the NGOMCS Study was published by Pequegnat et al. (1990). The scope of this review was comprehensive, providing overviews of the environment, the meiofauna, the macrofauna, the megafauna, and what was known at the time regarding chemosynthetic seep communities. The overview

1

focused on the apparent confirmation of the zonation scheme that had been previously postulated by Pequegnat (1983). The five faunal zones proposed by Pequegnat (1983) had been challenged by Carney et al. (1983). These authors had opined that faunal assemblages change continually with depth such that a distinct upper slope or shelf fauna penetrates to about 1,000-m depths, a distinct deep slope fauna is present below 2,000 m, and a broad transition zone occurs between 1,000-and 2,000-m depths. Pequegnat et al. (1990) rejected this view, but it must be acknowledged that the analysis format used to reject the view were not suitable for evaluating the Carney et al. (1983) hypothesis.

Offshore oil and gas exploration and development on the continental slope did not accelerate until the late 1990s. This resulted in a renewed interest in the continental slope ecosystem, and researchers rediscovered the NGOMCS study. However, it was also learned that the NODC database from this study had been lost or corrupted (Carney 2001), and the 48,000 benthic photographs were also lost. We, however, had retained hard copies of the data as well as duplicate photography. Under contract to MMS, we reconstructed the database and updated it to include revisions from work that occurred after the original study was completed. The updated database and the archived photographs were submitted to MMS and have been made available to a new MMS-sponsored deep-sea study being conducted by Texas A&M University.

This paper is primarily intended to provide a summary of some of the key NGOMCS Study findings, and also includes some new analyses addressing the zonation concept. We address the question of whether 1) there are three distinct megafaunal assemblages represented between the shelf edge and about 1,000 to 1,200 m, and that within each of these the fauna is homogeneous (i.e. does not change with depth); or 2) whether the fauna changes with depth in such a way that the general pattern of change is that of a nonrepeating sequence of species arrayed along the depth gradient.

While, theoretically, sampling had been targeted to occur at the mid-point of a defined biological zone, a much broader depth range of depths was typically sampled than was planned. We assigned samples to evenly-spaced 100-m depth intervals between 300 m and 3,000 m, and had good coverage for each of these depth intervals between 300 and 1,200 m. The primary question we address below is whether there are three distinct and homogeneous biological zones represented between 300 m and 1,000 to 1,200 m or whether the biota changes continually with depth. Both the Pequegnat et al. (1990) and Carney et al. (1983) viewpoints include a monotonous environment and biota between 1,000+ m to 2,000+ m where the fauna changes abruptly.

APPROACH AND METHODS

The sampling program of the NGOMCS Study was structured to test whether the abundance and composition of the biota on the continental slope varied in response to changes in any of several spatial, temporal, or physiochemical variables.

Analytical Design

A major component of the analytical design was the location of sampling stations. Sampling stations were located between the 200-m and 2,900-m isobaths on the continental slope of the northern Gulf of Mexico between about 86° and 94° west longitude (Fig. 1). Station locations by depth reflected the desire to compare fauna among depths and thus test the depth-zonation concept; sampling locations east and west of a central Gulf transect were intended to characterize the different OCS planning regions.

Three series of sampling stations, or transects, one in each MMS lease planning area, formed the nucleus of the sampling plan. (Additional areas were eventually sampled, for reasons to be discussed later.) Some characteristics of these three transects and the planning areas they represented are as follows:

1. Central Lease Planning Area—The transect representing this area extended across the slope in the vicinity of the Mississippi Trough, from approximately 28°20'N, 89°40'W to 26°40'N, 89°20'W (Fig. 1). The area has extremely active sediment movement, relatively high terrigenous inputs, and few striking topographic features; it is occasionally bathed by the Loop Current.

2. Western Lease Planning Area—The transect in this area extended across the slope just south of the Flower Garden Banks, from 27°25'N, 93°40'W to 25°50'N, 93°30'W (Fig. 1). The area has relatively sluggish circulation, a number of pronounced topographic features, and moderate to low declivity compared to the Mississippi Trough Transect.

3. Eastern Lease Planning Area—The sampling transect crossed the Florida Escarpment from 27°40'N, 85°15'W to 27°30'N, 85°40'W (Fig. 1). The area has high declivity (especially on the lower slope), a low rate of terrigenous input and sedimentation, and moderate to strong currents along the face of the slope.

Various combinations of these transects were sampled on Cruises I, II, and III. Cruises IV and V sampled additional areas in the eastern and western Gulf, respectively (Fig. 1). Descriptions of the sampling efforts on each cruise, and the rationale for such efforts, are described below.

On Cruise I (fall 1983), five stations at five different depths were sampled on the central transect (Fig. 1). The primary purpose of Cruise I was to collect samples within previously-defined faunal zones over a wide depth range (300 to 2,400 m) as a basis for refining future sampling efforts.

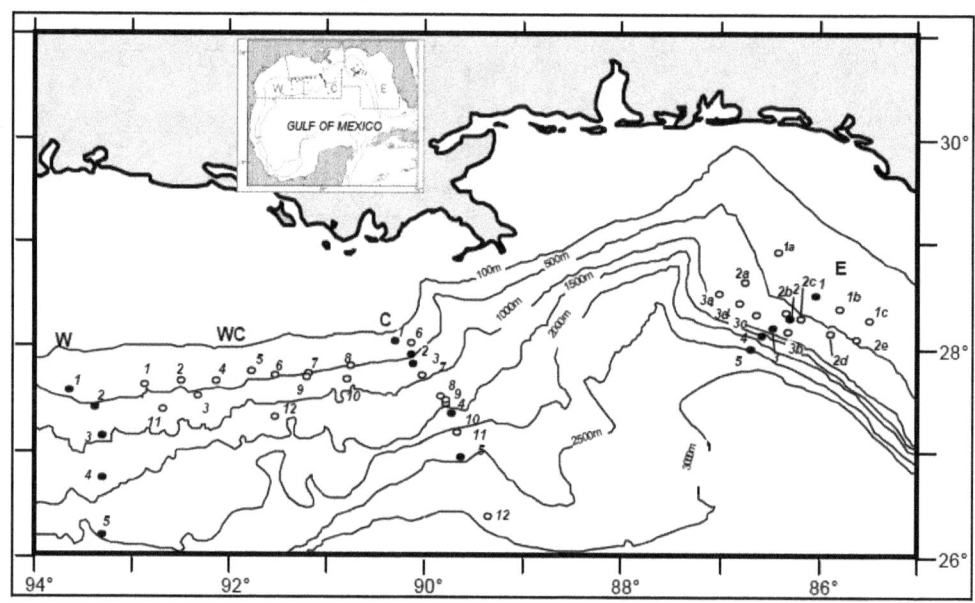

Figure 1. Sample sites in the Gulf of Mexico.

Cruise II (spring/summer 1984) re-sampled the stations occupied on Cruise I and also extended the geographic coverage to the western and eastern regions of the Gulf (Fig. 1). Cruise II results provided data for comparisons among planning areas and depths, and for stations on the central transect, between seasons.

During Cruise III (fall 1984), the five original central transect stations were sampled again in fall 1984, along with seven additional stations (Fig. 1). The seven new stations were located on the central transect at different depths from the first five stations. The locations for the additional stations were mainly in suspected biological "transition" areas and were based upon the advice of the program's Scientific Advisory Committee. Sampling the five original central transect stations allowed comparisons to be made between the fall cruise of 1983 and that of 1984.

During Cruise IV (spring/summer 1985), 16 stations were sampled near and on the eastern transect, including those previously occupied on the eastern transect on Cruise II (Fig. 1). The new stations were grouped by depth at approximately 350 m (four stations), 625 m (six stations), 850 m (five stations), and 2900 m (one station). The purpose of this grouping design was to test depth-related differences against variability related to distance along these isobaths. Annual variability could also be studied by comparing the data from Stations E1, E2, E3, and E5 on Cruise IV (Fig. 1) to data from Cruise II (Fig. 1) from the same stations a year earlier.

Station locations for Cruise V (spring/summer 1985) (Fig. 1) were chosen on the basis of two major needs. First, the area of sampling between the western and central transects was subject to ongoing and expected future oil and gas exploration and development activities, and many sites were selected along depth contours in this area to document longitudinal variability in sediment and biological characteristics. Second, hydrocarbon seeps had been reported in the area, and the associated biota had not been well documented. Two suspected areas of hydrocarbon seeps (Stations WC6 and WC7) were chosen to compare with probable "control" (non-seep) areas at comparable depths (Stations WC8 and WD2). Further, samples at WC11 (a topographic high feature 1,226 m deep) were compared to samples at WC12 (a topographic depression 1,236 m deep).

The sampling strategy described above permitted project scientists to make the following contrasts:

	Contrast	Data Source
ANOVA 1	Seasonal, geographic, and annual variation by depth	Central Transect, Cruises I & II Western, Central, and Eastern Transects, Cruise II; Central Transect, Cruises I & III
ANOVA 2	Zonation Patterns	Central Transect, Cruise III, plus data from all other cruises
ANOVA 3	Variation within depths, Western Gulf	West-Central Cruise V
ANOVA 4	Variation within depths, Eastern Gulf	Eastern Transect, Cruise IV

These sampling design considerations allowed researchers to analyze faunal distributions and abundance in space and time. Additional relationships of interest were the influences of sediment size, presence and types of hydrocarbons, and water quality on faunal distribution and abundance. Sediments and hydrocarbons were analyzed from the same samples from which meiofauna and macrofauna were analyzed; this allowed for comparisons among these physical variables and these faunal groups. Water quality was analyzed from samples taken along sampling transects providing data to compare with faunal characteristics of those transects.

Field Methods

Hydrographic Measurements

Continuous and discrete measurements of hydrographic parameters were obtained throughout the water column (surface to bottom) at five stations on each cruise. A Neil-Brown Mark III CTD/Rosette/Transmissometer System was used to obtain continuous data and discrete water samples. Continuous conductivity (salinity), temperature, depth, and transmission records were provided by the Neil-Brown CTD. At each station, a 12-bottle rosette attached to the CTD was used to collect 12 discrete water samples for measurements of temperature, salinity, dissolved oxygen, nutrients, and particulate organic carbon. Bottles were spaced throughout the water column in order to delineate the major water masses at each site. The CTD/Rosette/Transmissometer System was deployed with a pinger so that the cast could be safely lowered to within a few meters of the bottom. This was done in order to discern whether there were bottom nepheloid layers at each site.

Box Core Sampling (Meiofauna/Macrofauna)

Box core samples were taken at each station to obtain material for macroinfauna and meiofauna identification, sediment grain size, carbonate, total organic carbon, carbon isotopes, and hydrocarbons. Six replicate samples were taken at each station, except on the western and eastern transect stations during Cruise II, when only three replicates were taken per station. The replicates were then subdivided to provide material for the various types of analyses.

Box corers were deployed in yoked pairs, using a TAMU-modified version of the Gray-O'Hara modification of the J&O box corer (Fig. 2). On many occasions, only one cast was required to collect two replicates. The box corer measured 24.5 x 24.5 x 44 cm. It was fitted with a hinged door to prevent washout of samples, and had up to 135 kg of ballast. The door was open until the device had penetrated the substrate, whereupon the jaws and the door closed. The amount of ballast was adjusted to ensure adequate substrate penetration.

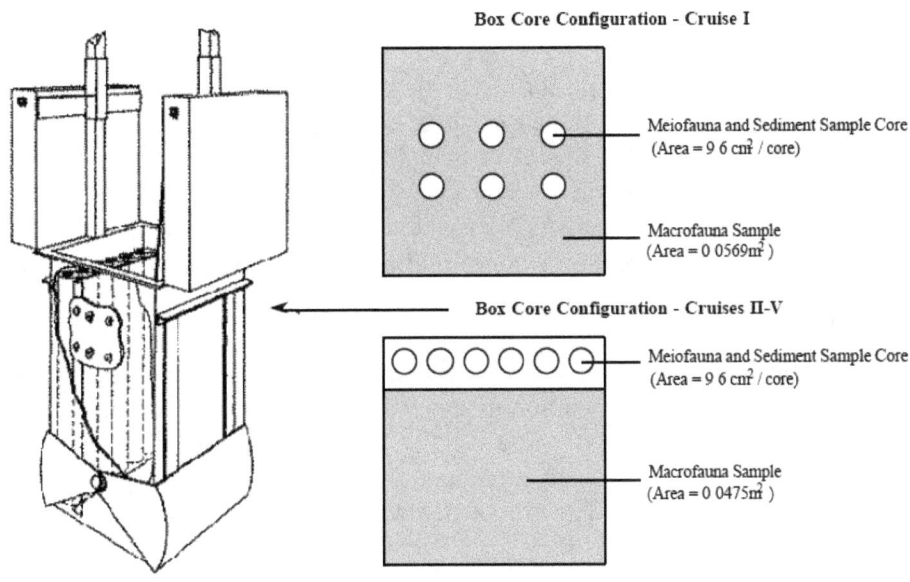

Figure 2. Box core and configuration of *in situ* subsampling tubes in the box corer.

The box corer contained six metal coring tubes, 43.5 cm long and 3.5 cm in internal diameter. During Cruise I, these tubes were mounted in three pairs on a wire rack in the center of the box. This design was improved on successive cruises by mounting all six tubes against one wall of the box and securing them behind an aluminum partition that extended the full depth of the box. As each box corer came onboard, the overlying water was carefully siphoned into the macrofauna container, and the remaining subsamples processed according to their intended uses.

Trawl Sampling (Megafauna)

Megafauna sampling was performed with a standard 9-m, semi-balloon otter trawl with 60-cm steel doors, 3.8-cm stretch mesh, and 1.3-cm cod end mesh. Target trawling times were one hour at stations shallower than 1300 m, and two or more hours at deeper stations. The amount of time on the bottom was arbitrarily measured as the time from winch brake application until the winch was started again for trawl retrieval. At a towing speed of one to three knots, a ratio (scope) of 3.5:1 between amount of wire out and the depth produced good samples.

The contents of each retrieved trawl were dumped into metal tubs. Fishes and invertebrates intended for hydrocarbon assays were quickly removed, photographed, and frozen. The remaining organisms were usually rough-sorted into three categories (fish, decapods, and "other"). They were then narcotized with isotonic magnesium sulfate if necessary, and preserved in 10% neutral buffered formalin in sea water.

Benthic Photography (Megafauna)

Benthic photographs were taken with the use of a Benthos Model 372 deep-sea camera fitted with a 28-mm lens (angle of view 35° x 48.5°), and equipped with a 200 watt-second (Joule) Benthos strobe. On each visit to every station, the camera exposed 800 frames of Kodak Ektachrome Professional 5936 film, ISO 200. Photographs were taken every eight seconds.

The photographic gear was mounted inside a protective framework (Fig. 3). This framework had a clock and altimeter that recorded the time and altitude above the bottom in the corner of each photograph. The altimeter had a resolution of ± 0.1 m.

The camera system was suspended from the vessel by a hydrographic wire, and allowed to drift near the bottom along transects 1500 to 5000 m long. This technique prevented skipping and bouncing on the bottom, thereby minimizing disturbance and reducing the chances of attracting or frightening animals away.

Altitude was maintained by adjusting the vessel's winch in response to an acoustic signal transmitted by a 12 kHz bottom-finding pinger on the framework. The signal was portrayed continuously on a strip chart recorder. Optimum camera altitude was approximately 2 m above the bottom, which produced shots that included 2.27 m^2 of the

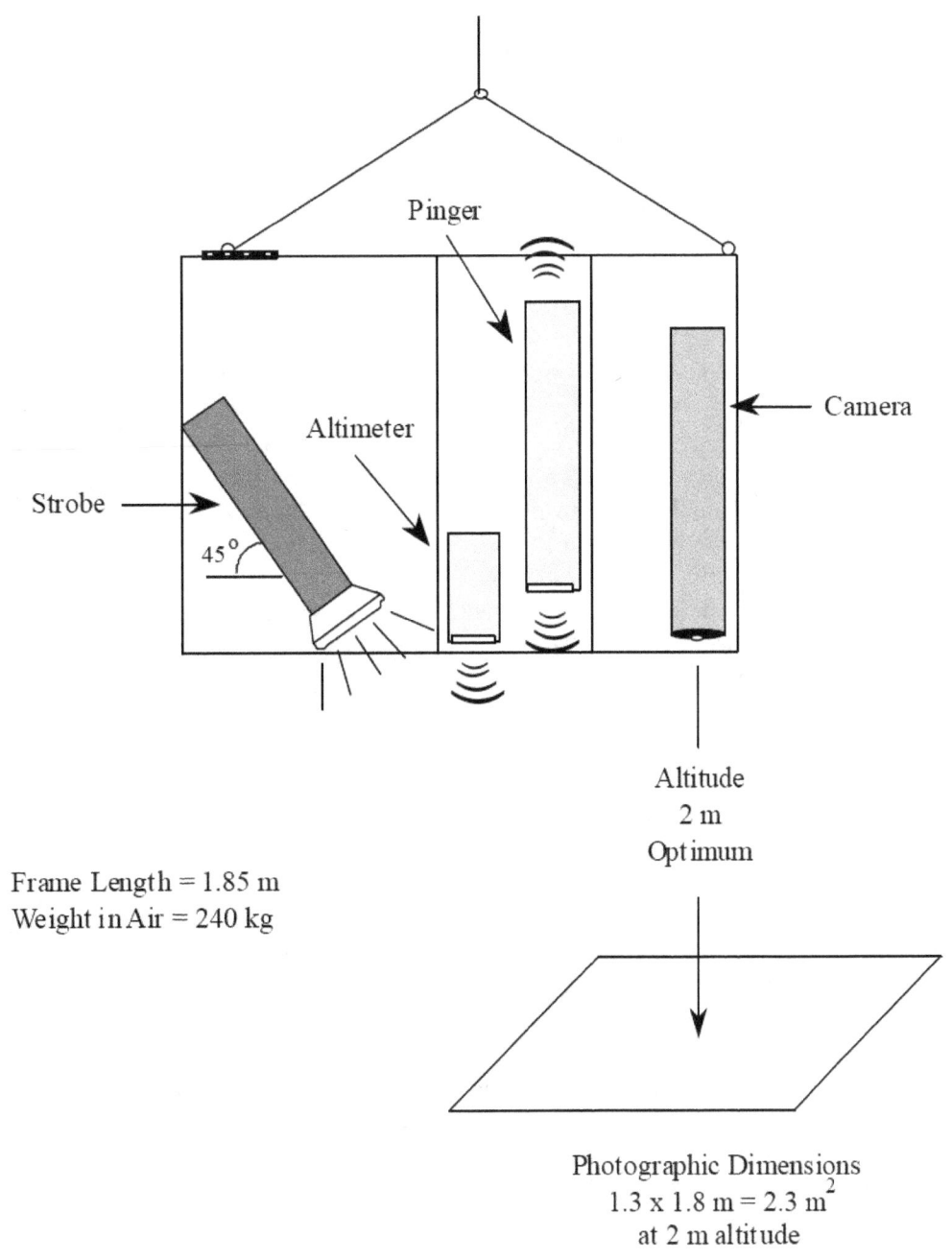

Pinger

Camera

Strobe

Altimeter

45°

Frame Length = 1.85 m
Weight in Air = 240 kg

Altitude
2 m
Optimum

Photographic Dimensions
1.3 x 1.8 m = 2.3 m^2
at 2 m altitude

Figure 3. Schematic diagrams of photographic system used for benthic photography.

bottom. However, acceptable shots were obtained at altitudes from 0.7 m (0.27 m² area) to 4.0 m (9.09 m² area).

Laboratory Methods

Laboratory activities included (1) analyzing sediments and biota for physical, chemical, and hydrocarbon parameters and for carbon isotope ratios; (2) sorting, identifying, enumerating, weighing, and measuring biota and analyzing their gut contents; and (3) analyzing photographs for biota and lebenspurren. Standard methods were used throughout each analysis and were detailed in Gallaway (1988b).

In the NGOMCS study, meiofauna were defined as those metazoan organisms retained on a 0.063-mm sieve after the sample had been rinsed through a 0.300-mm sieve to remove larger macrofaunal organisms. Biomass of meiofauna was estimated using published values for the size ranges and types of organisms in the samples (Fauble 1982, Rowe et al. 1974). Results were presented as densities per 10 cm² following Thiel (1983). Macrofauna were defined in the NGOMCS Study as those organisms collected in the box corer and retained on a 0.300-mm sieve. Representatives of four taxonomic groups (Nematoda; Copepoda, primarily harpacticoid copepods; Aplacophora; and Scyphozoa) were not included as macrofauna in the NGOMCS Study despite being retained on a 0.300-mm sieve. We include these forms in our synthesis as they constitute a significant fraction of the macrofaunal density and biomass that is not measured elsewhere.

Perhaps the most difficult aspect of the laboratory component of the study was the identification of the macrofauna. Our technicians field-collected and then sorted the collections to major taxonomic groups in the laboratory. With the exception of the polychaetes, we did not attempt to make any species-level identifications for any of the major groups represented in the collections. Rather, the rough-sorted samples were sent to an expert on the taxonomy of that group who made the species-level identifications. Overall, more than 30 taxonomic experts participated in the study (Fig. 4). Once identified, the samples and the data were returned to LGL. This process extended the time estimated necessary to identify the macrofauna by over one year. Nevertheless, the process yielded state-of-science level identifications, at least for that period in time.

Statistical Methods

Statistical treatment of the data included numerical classification (cluster analysis), calculation of diversity indices, and analysis of variance (ANOVA) on density values (Gallaway et al. 1988a; Gallaway 1988a, 1988b, 1988c). Also, correlation analyses (Pearsons product moment) were conducted, relating the density of the most abundant species to water and sediment quality variables.

TAXONOMIC EXPERTS

Nemertea - J. Wern (Texas A&M University)

Oligochaeta - C. Erseus (University of Goteborg)

Polychaeta - G.F. Hubbard (LGL), P. Wolfe &
       L. Sierte (B.A. Vittor & Assoc., Inc.)

Bivalvia - F. Rokop (Scripps Institute of Oceanography),
       T. Waller (Smithsonian Institution)

Cephalopoda - M. Sweeney (Smithsonian Institution)

Porifera - S. Pomponi (Consultant), D. La Chance (Consultant)

Actiniaria - D. Dunn Fautin (Calif. Academy of Sciences)

Alcyonaria - J. Lowery (Consultant), S. Viada (LGL)

Scleractinia - S. Cairns (Smithsonian Institution), S. Viada (LGL)

Hydrozoa - D. Calder (Royal Ontario Museum)

Gasteropoda - P. Bouchet (Museum National d'Historie Naturelle)

Scaphopoda - J. Kraeuter (Baltimore Gas and Electric)

Pycnogonida - C.A. Child (Smithsonian Institution)

Pogonophora - M. Jones (Smithsonian Institution)

Amphipoda - L. McKinney (Texas Parks and Wildlife)

Cirripedia - H. Spivey (Florida State University)

Cumacea - N. Jones (University of Liverpool)

Isopoda - G. Wilson (Consultant)

Ostracoda - L. Kornicker (Smithsonian Institution)

Stomatopoda - D. Camp (Florida Dept. Natural Resources)

Tanaidacea - R. Heard (Gulf Coast Research Lab)

Decapoda - L. & W. Pequegnat (Consultants), P. McLaughlin
       (Florida International University)

Asteroidea - D. Pawson (Smithsonian Institution)

Crinoidea - C. Messing (University of Miami)

Echinoidea - D. Pawson (Smithsonian Institution)

Holothuroidea - R. Carney (Louisiana State University)

Ophiuroidea - G. Hendler (LA County Museum of
       Natural History)

Brachiopoda - G.A. Cooper (Smithsonian Institution)

Bryozoa - A.J.J. Leuterman (Dresser Industries)

Sipunculida - M. Rice (Smithsonian Institution)

Tunicata - C. & F. Monniot (Museum National d'Historie
       Naturelle)

Fishes - C. Chandler (LGL), E. Matheson & J. McEachran
       (Texas A&M University)

Figure 4. Taxonomic experts involved in faunal identifications for the NGOMCS study.

Hurlbert's modification (1971) of the rarefaction method (Sanders 1968) was used to predict the number of species in a random sample without replacement, given a population N:

$$E(\hat{S}_m) = \sum_{i=1}^{k} \left[1 - \frac{\binom{N-N_i}{m}}{\binom{N}{m}} \right]$$

in which N_l is the finite population of species i; and $E(\hat{S}_m)$ is the variable denoting the expected number of species in a random sample of size m (Smith and Grassle 1977). N is the total number of individuals in the finite population:

$$\Sigma \, N_i$$

For the macrofauna species diversity results, we used m=50 or the number of species per 50 individuals; m=100 or the number of species per 100 individuals; m=500; m=1,000; m=2,000; and m=3,000. For megafauna diversity, we used m's ranging from 15 to 150.

ENVIRONMENTAL CHARACTERIZATION

One of the primary objectives of the NGOMCS Study was to describe the environment of the continental slope of the northern Gulf of Mexico in terms of overlying water masses, bottom water conditions, sedimentary character and hydrocarbon levels in the sediments. The overall purpose of this physical-chemical characterization was to identify spatial and temporal variations or discontinuities that might account for or be related to biological features. A major emphasis was placed upon the sources of, and the present levels of hydrocarbons in the sediments. Originally, this effort was perceived to be of most importance in that the data would constitute a pre-development baseline which could be used as a standard against which to compare the effects of hydrocarbon development on the continental slope. Sediment hydrocarbon levels were determined to influence biological communities of the slope, even when present in only trace amounts (Gallaway and Kennicutt 1988).

The primary water column difference between the Gulf of Mexico continental slope and other slope systems is that the shallow sill depth (~1900 m) at the Yucatan Strait connection between the Gulf and the Atlantic prevents the input of cold (2°C) bottom waters. As a result, slope habitats below 2000 m remain relatively warm (~4°C). Depth variation in temperature, salinity and dissolved oxygen exhibited classical and expected patterns and there were no, or only minimal, regional differences in these patterns.

Sediment characteristics did exhibit regional differences. The most common sediment type on the slope was silty clay, occurring in all geographic regions. However, in the eastern Gulf this general sediment type had higher percentages of sand than in the western or central areas of the Gulf. Clay sediments were found in the western and central Gulf but were not present in any of the eastern Gulf samples. In contrast, sand-silt-clay sediments were represented at some eastern Gulf stations but absent from the western Gulf stations. Sandy clay was found at shallow and deep stations in the western Gulf and at deep stations in the eastern Gulf.

Gulf of Mexico slope sediments contain a mixture of terrigenous, petroleum, and planktonic hydrocarbons. The influence of river/land derived material is widespread and is probably delivered to the slope by secondary sediment movement such as slumping and slope failure. Petroleum hydrocarbons were detected at all locations and have a dual source in natural seepage and river-associated transport. Other contemporary studies suggested that natural seepage is much more widespread on the Gulf of Mexico slope than previously thought and probably represents a significant input of petroleum hydrocarbon to Gulf slope sediments (Brooks et al. 1985, Lacerda et al. 1987, Kennicutt et al. 1987).

In general, the concentration of hydrocarbons in slope sediments (except in seep areas) was lower than previous reports for shelf and coastal sediments but no consistent decrease with increasing water depth was apparent below 300 m. Hydrocarbon distributions, in general, were observed to be patchy on the slope and this may have been due in part to the non-uniform distribution of natural seepage on the slope. Variability in hydrocarbon concentrations were as much as 1 to 2 orders of magnitude along an isobath, due to changes in sediment texture and hydrocarbon inputs. Hydrocarbons were preferentially associated with clayey, organic-rich sediments suggesting a linkage with river-derived material. Aromatic hydrocarbon concentrations were very low at all locations but their presence was confirmed by fluorescence analysis.

Megafaunal organisms collected from non-seep areas had variable levels of hydrocarbons in their tissues, mainly derived from the sediments either directly or from organisms that had ingested sediments (Gallaway and Kennicutt 1988). Hydrocarbons were more prevalent in fishes than in decapod crustaceans. Terrigenous hydrocarbons were common but the majority of the hydrocarbons appeared of plankton origin.

Results of the Principal Component Analyses (PCA) suggested distinct regional differences in slope habitats, with the central Gulf having the highest levels of total organic carbon and petroleum hydrocarbons and the lowest levels of sand in the sediments (Gallaway and Kennicutt 1988). The stations in the eastern Gulf had the lowest levels of organic carbon and hydrocarbons in slope sediments and the highest levels of sand. Stations along the western Gulf slope transect were intermediate between these extremes. Data from each regional transect suggested differences along the transect by depth, namely that the proportion of plankton-derived hydrocarbons and the petroleum indicator of high molecular weight hydrocarbons (PE-Hi) increased with depth and distance from shore. There was also an indication of higher organic carbon and petroleum levels associated with topographic irregularities that would enhance sediment accumulation.

Results of the PCA designed to evaluate depth differences suggested distinct differences in habitats by depth on the central transect. Three general habitats were indicated—shallow (<500-m deep), deep (>2000 m) and intermediate (500- to 2000-m deep). This suggests a distinct deep-shelf habitat, connected by a broad transition zone to a distinct abyssal habitat beginning at about 2000 m. Subsequent PCA's conducted on samples collected along isobaths suggested habitats along depth contours differed more by depth than along a depth contour.

BIOLOGICAL CHARACTERIZATION

Fifty-nine (59) of the 60 planned box core samples were obtained and analyzed. However, macrofaunal data from station C1, replicate 3 and C12, replicate 4 were lost to laboratory error (samples were sorted to major group, but improperly preserved and then deteriorated prior to identification). Similarly, 59 of the 60 planned trawl tows were taken but an additional 14 of the tows experienced problems such that the data collected could not be considered quantitative (Appendix 1). A total of 45 quantitative tows were obtained. None of the benthic photography samples from Cruise I (5 stations) yielded quantitative data. However, quantitative data were obtained from all other cruise and station combinations.

The overall distribution of biological sampling effort by depth is shown by Table 1. Reasonable coverage was obtained for all gear types to depth intervals between 300 and 1,500 m. Little or no sampling was conducted using any gear between 1,600 and 2,000 m, and limited box core, photographic, and trawl sampling was conducted between 2,100 and 3,000 m.

Meiofauna

The meiofauna collections contained in excess of 230,000 individuals representing 43 major groups of animals (Gallaway et al. 1988b). However, representatives of five taxa of permanent meiofauna (Nematoda, Harpacticoida, Polychaeta, Ostracoda, and Kinorhyncha) along with naupliar larvae (temporary meiofauna) comprised 98% of the collections. Numerically the collections were dominated by nematodes and harpacticoids, but on a biomass basis polychaetes and ostracods were dominant. This structure was remarkably consistent across all stations, regions, seasons, and years (Gallaway et al. 1988b).

From inspection of the overall density patterns, meiofaunal abundance appeared somewhat greater in spring than in fall and higher on the central transect than on the eastern and western transects. Also, there was an overall trend of decrease in abundance with depth, but this was not always the case.

Table 1

Distribution of Total Area Sampled by Gear Type and Depth Interval

Depth Interval	Box Core (m^2)	Camera (ha)	Trawl (ha)
300	1.206	0.165	10.744
400	1.748	0.316	15.616
500	0.950	0.203	10.077
600	3.571	0.351	24.985
700	0.238	0.166	5.330
800	1.871	0.308	33.522
900	1.368	0.188	11.285
1000	0.285	0.055	
1100	0.095	0.047	6.413
1200	0.713	0.117	7.787
1300	0.209	0.078	
1400	1.130	0.102	10.744
1500	0.238		
1600		0.057	
1700			
1800			
1900			
2000			
2100	0.285	0.055	
2200			
2300			
2400	0.285	0.086	5.663
2500	0.769	0.029	5.122
2600			
2700			
2800	0.095		
2900	0.475	0.136	
3000	0.143		

A more detailed examination of depth distribution was enabled from the fall 1984 sampling on the central transect. The results of this sampling also suggest a general decline in abundance with depth with notable exceptions to the pattern exhibited at Stations C7 and C4. The former station had anomalously high petroleum hydrocarbon levels and was documented to have had a population of chemosynthetic bivalves.

Relatively little variation was observed along isobaths sampled in the eastern and western Gulf of Mexico, and little across-isobath variation was noted for the depth intervals sampled on these cruises. The samples reflected remarkable constancy.

Mean density of meiofauna across all stations in this study was 700 organisms/10 cm^2, with individual station values ranging from about 200 to 1,100 organisms/10 cm^2. In general these counts appear higher than comparable meiofaunal values for the western Atlantic (Wigley and McIntyre 1964, Tietjen 1971, and Coull et al. 1977 as shown in Thiel 1983). There, maximum values were on the order of 100 to 400 individuals/10 cm^2. Sieve sizes used in the referenced western Atlantic samples ranged from 0.042 to 0.074 mm as compared to the 0.063 mm sieve used in this study. From this comparison we conclude that the Gulf meiofaunal densities are greater than those of the U.S. Atlantic. In fact, review of the data presented in Thiel (1983) suggests that the meiofaunal densities observed in this program are among the highest recorded in any deep-sea habitat.

Both macrofauna and meiofauna numbers and biomass decreased overall with depth. For the macrofauna, numbers declined less rapidly than biomass, suggesting that macrofaunal size decreased with depth (Fig. 5). For the meiofauna, numbers also declined less rapidly than biomass but the difference between the two slopes was marginal, suggesting little change in size. In contrast to Thiel's (1983) findings, we observed densities of meiofauna to decline at a more rapid rate than densities of macrofauna (ratio between meio- to macrofaunal slopes was 1.67 to 1 as compared to 0.5 to 1 in Thiel). However, the macrofauna were screened using a 0.300 mm sieve in our program, whereas Rowe (1971) used a screen size of 0.42 mm in his studies. Rowe's (1971) results formed the basis for Thiel's comparison.

Because of the gross level of taxonomy used (and available) for the meiofauna, detailed correlations were considered unwarranted. However, some observations were made. As noted above, significant exceptions to the tend of decreasing density of meiofauna with depth were observed. These included Stations C4 and C7 sampled on the central transect in fall 1984. Station C7 had enriched levels of petroleum hydrocarbons and benthic photographs revealed a dense community of chemosynthetic clams in the surface sediments. This may be indicative that when localized chemical enrichment of sediments provides the basis for a chemosynthetic food web, a general increase in infaunal density and diversity may occur in the larger area.

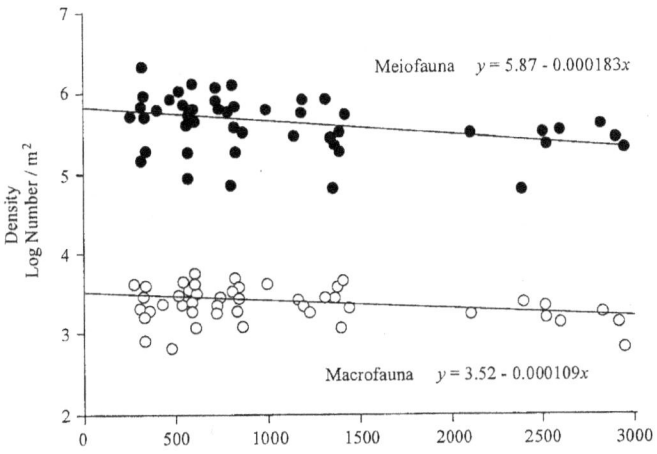

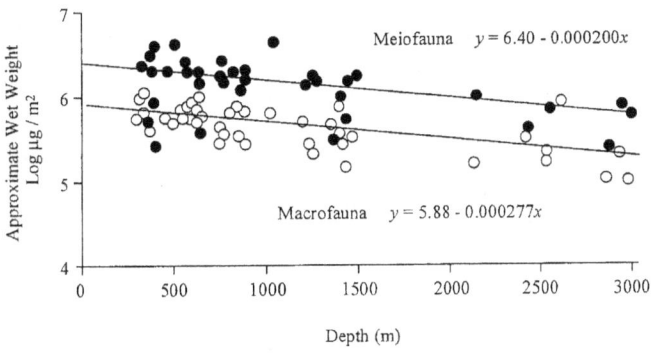

Figure 5. Relative occurrence of meiofauna and macrofauna with depth at all sampling stations in terms of density and approximate biomass. (Source Gallaway et al. 1988a).

Some 500 specimens of the phylum Loricifera were collected during the NGOMCS Study at depths ranging from 298 to 2,959 m (Hubbard et al. 1988). They were collected from all but four of the stations sampled. This phylum was only described in 1983 (Kristensen 1983) based upon specimens collected from near Roscoff, France; the Azores; and near Fort Pierce, Florida at depths ranging from 15 to 480 m. Specimens of this phylum were reported by Kristensen to be generally overlooked since a species shock treatment with freshwater was required to effectively dislodge them from marine sediments. One must wonder how many might have been collected if our samples had been treated accordingly. In any case, the NGOMCS Study findings substantially increase both the geographic and depth ranges for the Loricifera.

The meiofauna of the Gulf of Mexico were poorly known at the time of the NGOMCS Study and remain so. However, meiofaunal densities on the continental slope of the Gulf were high in the mid 1980s and rivaled or exceeded the macrofauna in biomass, attesting to the small size of Gulf macrofauna. The patterns of abundance as compared to the macrofauna lend credence to the idea that, in comparison to other slope systems, food or energy availability in the Gulf may be low, thereby limiting population density levels.

Macrofauna

A total of 69,933 organisms representing in excess of 1,548 differentiable taxa were obtained by the NGOMCS Study (Table 2). It should be noted that we have included some forms generally considered as meiofauna (e.g., Nematoda, Harpacticoida, Cyclopoidea) in the macrofaunal counts. Larger specimens of these groups were retained on the 0.300-mm screen and, if not included in the macrofauna counts, would not be represented in any of the samples. These forms constitute up to half or more of the total density and biomass of the slope infauna. One characteristic of the Gulf-slope macrofauna which was remarked upon by many of the taxonomic experts who identified the species within groups was their small size as compared with the western North Atlantic.

The taxonomic experts were able to identify 1,107 species within the 46 major groups. Polychaetes were represented by 405 species, tanadaceans were represented by 168 species and 119 species of isopods were identified (Table 2). Selective and non-selective deposit feeders (196 taxa) dominated the polychaete collections in terms of total counts and number of taxa. However, more families of carnivorous polychaetes were collected than families or any other category, but their abundances were less than either deposit feeders or omnivores (Pequegnat et al. 1990). Scavengers were the least abundant of any of the polychaete feeding types.

Overall, macrofaunal density appeared to decline with depth, especially between 1,000 to 3,000 m (Fig. 6). However, there was a large gap in sampling effort between 1,500 and 2,100 m. There was no marked trend of decline between 300 and 1,500 m

Table 2

Relative Abundance of Major Macrofaunal Groups

Taxonomic Group	Abundance	Number of Taxa	Number of Species	Number of Genera	Number of Other Taxa
Polychaeta	24,547	601	405	151	45
Nematoda	17,020	1			1
Ostracoda	4,931	22	18	1	3
Harpacticoida	3,727	1			1
Bivalvia	3,648	55	41	10	4
Tanaidacea	3,579	186	168	13	5
Bryozoa	3,043	99	82	12	5
Isopoda	2,372	133	119	8	6
Amphipoda	1,277	76	49	10	17
Aplacophora	871	1			1
Nemertini	645	20	19		1
Ophiuroidea	602	17	13	3	1
Sipuncula	568	36	30	3	3
Cumacea	508	85	75	8	2
Porifera	416	39	21	11	7
Scaphopoda	381	10	5	2	3
Scyphozoa	331	1			1
Gastropoda	278	52	8	26	18
Holothuroidea	249	13	4	4	5
Oligochaeta	248	9	6	1	2
Ascidiacea	135	18	11	3	4
Hydrozoa	102	15	8	3	4
Brachiopoda	79	2	2		
Halacaridae	62	1			1
Kinorhyncha	60	3		2	1
Echinoidea	49	6	3	1	2
Priapulida	33	1			1
Scleractinia	33	6	4	1	1
Cyclopoida	28	1			1
Decapoda	25	13	10	1	2
Mystacocarida	12	1			1
Pogonophora	11	1			1
Echiura	9	1			1
Actiniaria	8	3			3
Alcyonaria	8	2	1		1
Turbellaria	8	1			1
Crinoidea	7	2	2		
Pycnogonida	7	4	3	1	
Anthozoa	4	2			2
Hemichordata	4	1			1
Asteroidea	2	2		1	1
Mysidacea	2	1			1
Archiannelida	1	1			1
Cephalochordata	1	1			1
Cirripedia	1	1			1
Osteichthyes	1	1			1
	69,933	1,548	1,107	276	165

19

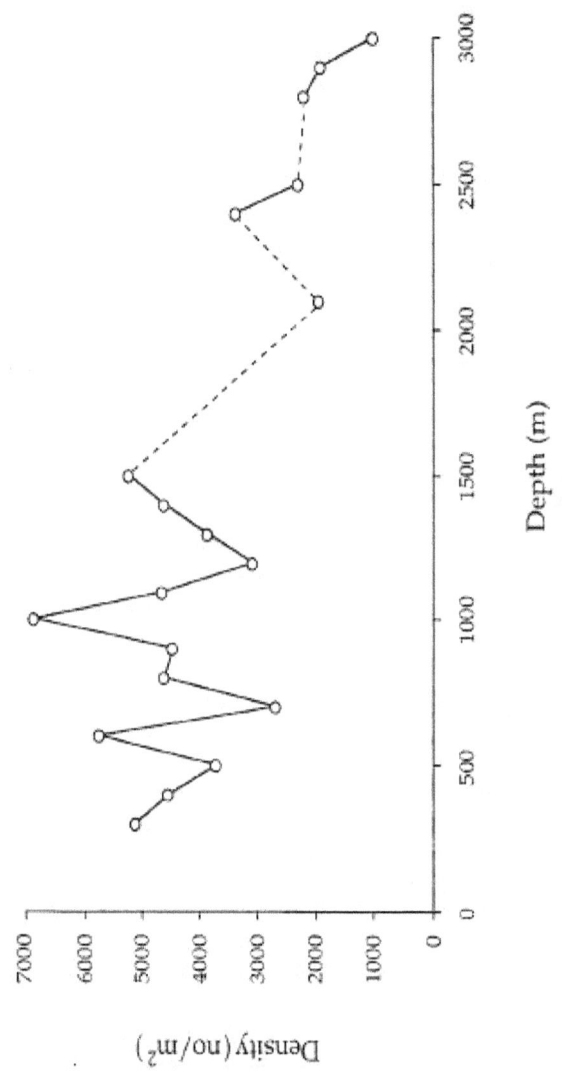

Figure 6. Macrofauna density by depth.

(peak abundance occurred at 1,000 m) nor was there a trend of decline between 2,100 and 2,900 m. However, the densities in the later region were substantially lower than observed densities between 300 and 1,500 m. The actual pattern of the decline between these two depths was not documented. The lowest density was observed at 3,000 m. Overall, the decline of macrofaunal abundance with depth fits a linear model ($p<0.0001$, $r^2 = 0.58$), especially for the depth region between the 1,000-m peak and the 3,000-m low.

As noted in Pequegnat et al. (1990), macrofaunal abundance (excluding nematodes and copepods) was higher in spring than in fall and, in spring, higher on the central transect (x = 3,437 individuals/m^2) than on the eastern (x = 2,878 individuals/m^2), and western transects (x = 2,189 individuals/m^2). Note that these numbers differ somewhat from the values shown in Pequegnat et al.'s (1990) Figure 4. The changes reflect corrections and updates made to the data after program completion.

Total macrofaunal density patterns based on all macrofauna (including nematodes and copepods) also showed higher abundance in spring than in fall. In spring, abundance on the central (x = 4,938 individuals/m^2) and eastern transects (x = 4,869 individuals/m^2) were similar and higher than abundance on the western transect (x = 3,389 individuals/m^2). Note that densities including total organisms retained on the 0.300-mm mesh screen are some 1.4 to 1.7 times higher than the densities reflected when large specimens of meiofaunal taxa (e.g., nematodes and copepod) are not included.

Thirteen species of polychaetes were included in the list of 18 macrofaunal species which constituted as much as 2% of the total macrofaunal collection (Table 3). Of these 13 species, three (*Litocorsa antennata*, *Pholoe* "Sp. C", and *Fauveliopsis* Sp. B) exhibited high abundance at depths between 300 and 1,000 m, and one (*Muldane*, "Sp. A) was more abundant at deeper (> 1000 m) as opposed to shallower depths (300-900 m). The remaining nine species exhibited variable but generally high abundance across the entire depth range sampled, at least to 1,500 m.

Observed diversity of macrofauna on the continental slope of the Gulf was high. The 1,107 species identified were represented by a total of 28,609 specimens. There were 972 species in 22,604 specimens collected at depths $\leq$ 1,000 m and 604 species contained in 6,005 specimens collected at depths greater than 1,000 m. The results of rarefaction analysis of these data were:

Subsample	All Depths Mean No. Species	Depth $\leq$ 1,000 m Mean No. Species	SD	Depth > 1,000 m Mean No. Species	SD
50	39.56	38.42	2.85	36.46	2.90
100	68.74	66.31	4.21	64.18	4.22
500	207.28	195.45	8.10	195.20	7.84
750	263.22	247.01	9.05	247.00	8.56
1000	308.96	289.16	9.66	288.38	8.93
2000	439.51	409.63	10.82	402.13	9.04
3000	527.82	491.35	11.20	474.89	8.33

Table 3

Density (no/m^2) of the 13 Polychaetes that Comprised as Much as 2% of the Total Macrofaunal Collection
(Bold line represents high density zone)

Polychaeta Species	300	400	500	600	700	800	900	1000	1100	1200	1300	1400	1500
Litocorsa antennata	268	130	249	116		4	4						
Pholoe "Sp. C"	17	26	9	54		59	35	4					
Levinsenia gracilis	39	39	52	35	38	22	10	14		8	5	9	8
Fauveliopsis Sp. B	22	27	4	20	8	20	29	4	21	22	10	10	4
Aricidea suecica	45	54	27	27	4	15	32	39		3	62	27	42
Aurospio dibranchiata	153	144	46	90	17	85	75		126	28		36	93
Prionospio ehlersi	41	70	88	25	8	10	9	4	32	1		6	25
Sarsonuphis hartmanae	16	16	33	37	17	11	13	4	21	15	19	8	17
Spiophanes berkeleyorum	44	27	63	43	8	30	30	81	42	13	14	32	29
Tachytrypane Sp. A	48	52	87	67	17	14	14	25		3		4	13
Exogone "Sp. A"	7	17	17	37	13	36	29	32	32	11	72	44	67
Terebellides atlantis	5	19	12	38		33	55	25		4	14	19	42
Maldane "Sp. A"	1	2	3	1		2	3	1179	305	177	220	277	968

There was little difference in the number of species represented in a given subsample size between depths, except for the largest of the sample sizes. At large sample sizes, macrofauna were more diverse at depths less than 1,000 m than at deeper depths.

Densities of macrofauna observed at NGOMCS Study sampling sites were generally lower than densities observed in contemporary continental slope studies being conducted in the Atlantic (Maciolek-Blake et al. 1985, Maciolek et al. 1986), especially at depths shallower than 1,000 m (Fig. 7). The differences in density between the Gulf and the Atlantic were less pronounced at deeper depths. The implication is that density of macrofauna on the continental slope of the Gulf declines at a much lower rate than is the case along the north- and mid-Atlantic coasts of the U.S.

In contrast, diversity of macrofauna at sampling sites on the upper Gulf slope (< 1,000 m) was observed to be much higher than was observed at depths less than 1,000 m on the Atlantic slope (Fig. 8). However, between depths of 1,000 m and 2,000 m, the Atlantic rarefaction curves for macrofauna all fell within the envelope of Gulf macrofaunal rarefaction curves. Further, at depths between 2,000 m and 3,000 m, the Gulf curves all fell within the envelope of Atlantic curves (Fig. 8). Thus, the observed diversity difference between the Atlantic and the Gulf was restricted to depths shallower than 1,000 m, the same area where density differences were most pronounced. The shallow (< 1,000 m) Gulf slope was characterized by high diversity and low abundance as compared to the same region of the Atlantic slope which had relatively high density and low diversity.

Megafauna

The NGOMCS Study trawl collections contained 5,751 specimens of fish representing 153 taxa of which 124 were identified to species. The trawl collections contained about 6 times more invertebrates (33,695 specimens) than fish. The trawl collection of invertebrates contained some 538 taxa of which 392 were identified to species. The photographs taken during the NGOMCS Study contained some 517 fishes among which 76 taxa were delineated. In contrast, some 56,052 observations representing 193 taxa of non-fish organisms were photographed. The observed plants and invertebrates in the latter category ranged from bacterial mats, to sargassum weed to colonial and individual invertebrates. Of these, roughly one-half of the observations (28,393) were represented by pteropod (a pelagic gastropod) shells. The photographic samples were dominated by holothurians (11,423 observations), bivalves (2,832 specimens, mainly from a chemosynthetic clam bed), and alcynarians (1,744 specimens, mainly sea pens). None of these groups were amenable to effective sampling by trawling. In fact, not one of the dominant holothurian photographed throughout the study area (*Peniagone* sp.) was trawled.

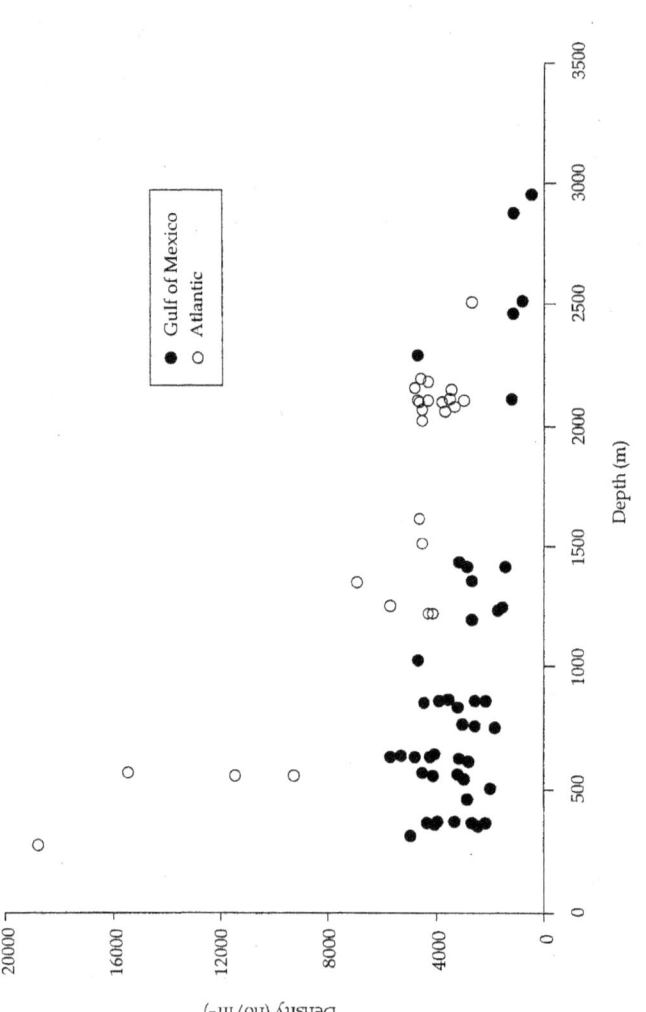

Figure 7.   Comparative density by depth of macrofauna for the Atlantic and Gulf of Mexico NGOMCS study sites. Atlantic data are from Maciolek-Blake et al. (1985) and Maciolek et al. (1986)

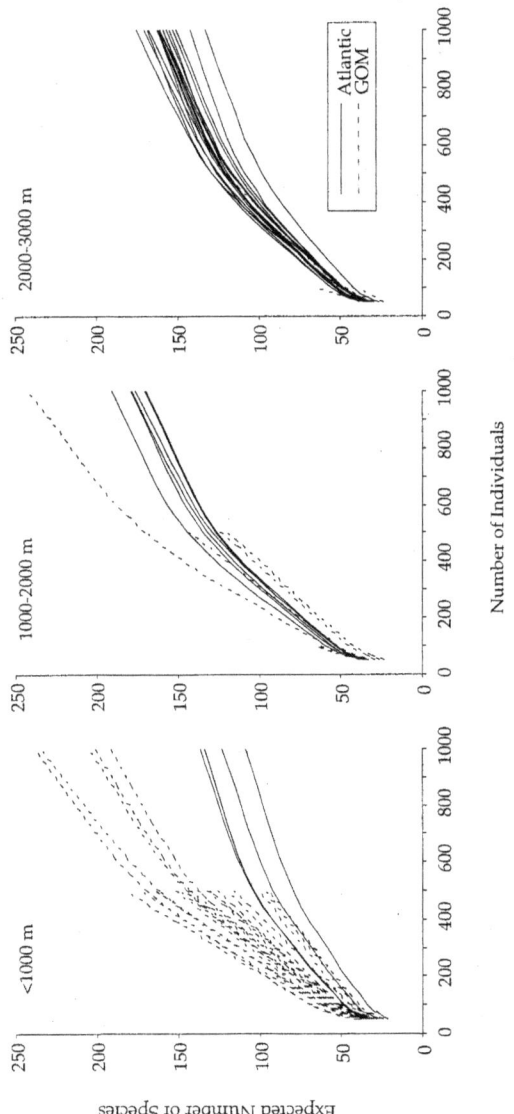

Figure 8. Number of expected species of macrofauna given the number of individuals in a sample for three depth strata in the North and Mid-Atlantic and the Gulf of Mexico. Each line represents an individual site. Atlantic data from Maciolek-Blake et al. (1985) and Maciolek et al. (1986).

25

Decapod crustaceans were the fourth most abundant major taxa in the benthic photographs and they dominated the trawl collections. Decapods and demersal fish are used as a basis for comparison of abundance trends represented by the two different sampling approaches.

Abundance and Diversity

Megafaunal invertebrate and fish densities were variable but high between depths of 300 and 1,200 m as compared to densities observed between 1,400 and 2,400 m (Figs. 9 and 10). Megafaunal invertebrate trawl densities increased at 2,500 m and a different species composition than was observed at shallower depths was associated with this increase. Holothurians were the dominant component. The trawl data (Fig. 9) reflect two peaks in invertebrate and fish abundance; the highest occurred at 500 m, and another but lower peak was evident between 1,100 and 1,200 m. The decline in abundance after 1,200 m was abrupt and abundance remained low down to 2,400 m. The overall trend is one of decline with depth, but the rate of decline is not necessarily consistent across all depths.

The densities of decapod crustaceans from both the trawl and photographic sampling reflected a pattern similar to that described for the total invertebrate collections (Fig. 10). Abundance was variable but generally declined with depth from between about 500 and 1,200 m, after which abundance was markedly lower than the peaks seen at shallower depths (Fig. 10). The fish density data showed an oscillating abundance pattern between 300 and 1,200 m followed by a step decline. Low abundance was characteristic of all sampling depths between 1,300 and 2,900 m.

The camera and trawl densities [transformed using $\log_e$ (n+1)] were regressed on depth and subjected to analysis of covariance. Both regressions were significant at $p \leq 0.001$ and the slopes of the two regressions were not significantly different. The regression of the transformed trawl decapod densities on camera densities was significant ($p = 0.0019$, $r^3 = 0.599$) with the relationships being expressed

$$\text{Log}_e \text{ (trawl density +1)} = -3.0859 + 1.1552 \log_e \text{ (camera density +1)}$$

Overall, the density of decapod crustaceans estimated from photographs was about 3.2 times higher than the density estimates reflected by trawling.

A similar analysis comparing trawl and photographic sampling results was conducted for the fish data. Significant regressions were obtained by depth, and the regressions had non-significant slope differences. The regression of trawl on camera density was significant ($p = 0.001$, $r^2 = 0.797$) with their relationship being expressed

$$\text{Log}_e \text{ (trawl density +1)} = -3.0251 + 1.1916 \times \log_e \text{ (camera density +1)}$$

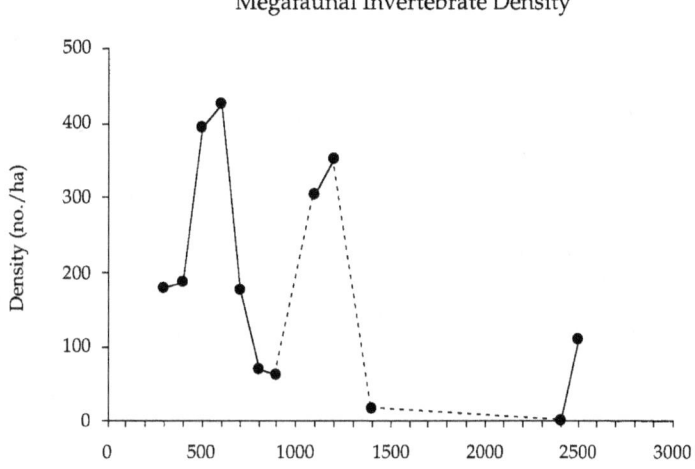

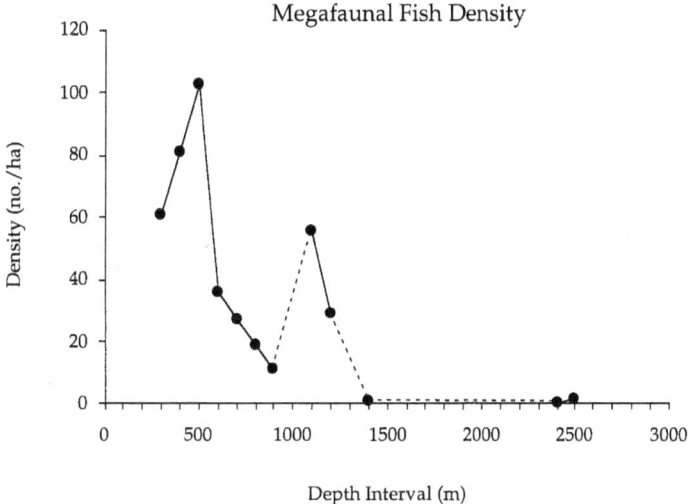

Figure 9. Megafaunal density by depth interval for the northern Gulf of
Mexico based upon trawls.

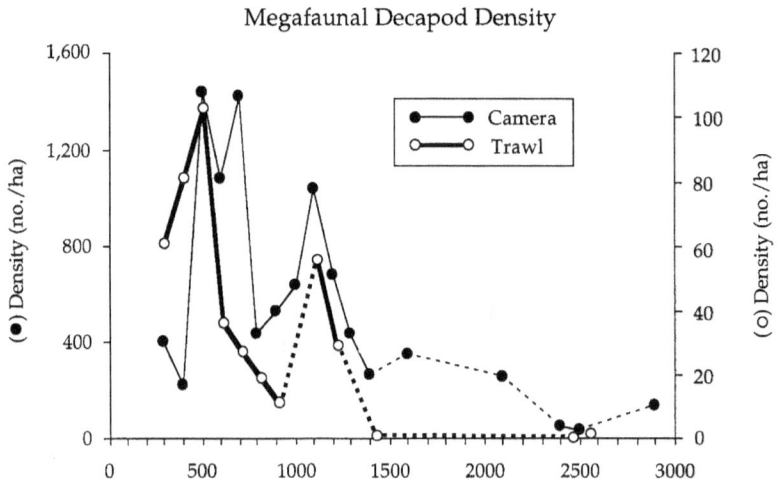

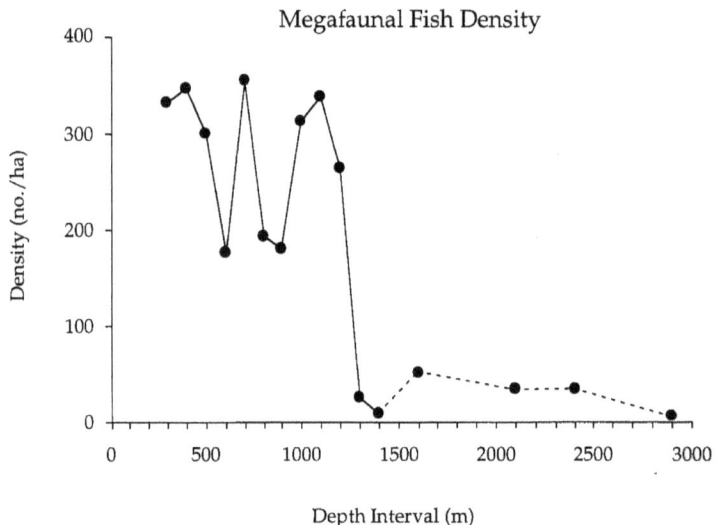

Figure 10. Megafaunal density by depth interval for the northern Gulf of Mexico based upon photographic observations and trawls.

Again, fish densities calculated from the photographic samples were, on average, about three times higher than calculated trawl densities.

There were nine species of decapod crustaceans which comprised as much as 2% of the total decapod trawl collections, and 12 species of fish which comprised as much as 2% of the total fish collections made by trawling. In each instance, these species showed sequentially overlapping depth distributions from 300 m down to 1,200 m, and none was abundant at 1,400 m (Table 4). Overall, the NGOMCS Study megafauna data support the idea that faunal composition changes continually with depth such that a distinct upper slope fauna penetrates to about 1,200-m depths and a distinct deep-slope fauna is present below 2,500 m. A broad transition zone characterized low abundance and diversity occurs between depths of 1,200 and 2,500 m.

Musick (1976) calculated Shannon-Weiner (H') diversity indices for fish collections taken on the U.S. Atlantic continental slope. Diversity was observed to decline with depth between 500 and 2,600 m. Shannon-Weiner fish diversity indices calculated from the NGOMCS Study data exhibited similar magnitudes of diversity as shown by Muscik (1976), and diversity at deeper stations was lower than diversity at shallower stations (Fig. 11). However, in the Gulf, diversity was high between 500 and 1,200 m and then exhibited a step decline. Below 1,200 m, diversity was uniform at about one-half the level observed at shallower depths (Fig. 11). The Musick (1976) data reflected a near linear or exponential decay in diversity with depth.

Results of rarefaction analysis did not reflect a decline in fish or megafaunal invertebrate diversity with depth between depths of 300 and 1,200 m (Fig. 12). For invertebrates, diversity at nine sampling depths between 300 and 1,200 m showed four groups of similar curves. The diversity levels for the three deepest depths (900; 1,100; and 1,200 m) fell among the highest observed (900 m), in the upper middle range (1,200 m) and at the lowest (1,100 m) level of observed diversities. The depth pattern for fish diversity between depths of 300 and 1,200 m was similar to that observed for megafaunal invertebrates. There was no evidence of a depth-related decline in diversity for this depth range (Fig. 12).

Life History Data

Life history data were taken for megafauna trawled at the 60 sampling stations. The specimens were first measured and weighed, and invertebrates were sexed and examined externally to determine the number of ovigerous females. Fish were dissected to determine food habits and state of maturity. As noted earlier, over 5,700 fish were collected, representing 124 species. However, most species were represented by fewer specimens than the number of trawls taken (60). Only five species were represented by more than 300 specimens, or on average as many as five specimens per trawl. Thus, while the data are of value because there is very little life history information concerning any of the species, they were not adequate to delineate trends or differences among regions, seasons, years, and depth.

Table 4

Densities of Abundant Decapod Crustaceans and Fish by Depth as Reflected by the Trawl Collections of the NGOMCS Study

Species	300	400	500	600	700	800	900	1000*	1100	1200	1300*	1400	1500*
Decapods													
Penaeopsis serrata	94.6	97.5	3.3										
Benthochascon schmitti	3.7	18.7	103	0.5		0.1							
Uroptychus nitidus		0.1	4.3	10.2	0.4	0.0	0.4		0.6	0.6		0.1	
Plesionika holthusi		0.6	7.5	52.3	11.1	0.7	0.4						
Munida valida			21.4	49.5	5.4	1.1	0.4			0.5			
Bathyplax typhla		0.1	38.6	60.2	37.7	2.5	0.4			0.6		0.6	
Nematocarcinus rotundus			0.2	54.1	9.9	10.2	8.2		159	36.3		1.0	
Stereomastis sculpta				3.8	1.1	7.7	5.3		10.4	12.1		0.7	
Glyphocrangon nobilis						0.1	0.1		40.2	5.5		1.0	
Fishes													
Coelorinchus caribbaeus	9.3	4.2				0.0							
Poecilopsetta beani	5.8	5.4		0.0		0.0							
Chloropthalmus agassizi	4.9	12.6	2.7										
Urophycis cirratus	7.1	6.4	18.0	0.7									
Bembrops goboides	6.1	14.0	6.5	0.2	0.2								
Epigonus pandionis	2.2	6.0	4.0	0.1	0.1								
Coelorinchus coelorhynchus	2.0	4.5	9.7	0.5	0.4								
Hymenocephalus italicus	0.3	14.0	6.5	0.2	0.2								
Dibranchus atlanticus		1.3	17.9	8.3	9.0	2.5	1.0						
Nezumia aegualis			0.6	5.9	3.0	1.2	1.2					0.1	
Synaphobranchus oregoni			0.1	1.1	0.6	5.0	2.7		7.5	2.7		0.1	
Gadomus longifilis						0.6	0.6		18.4	4.5			

*Depth interval not sampled.

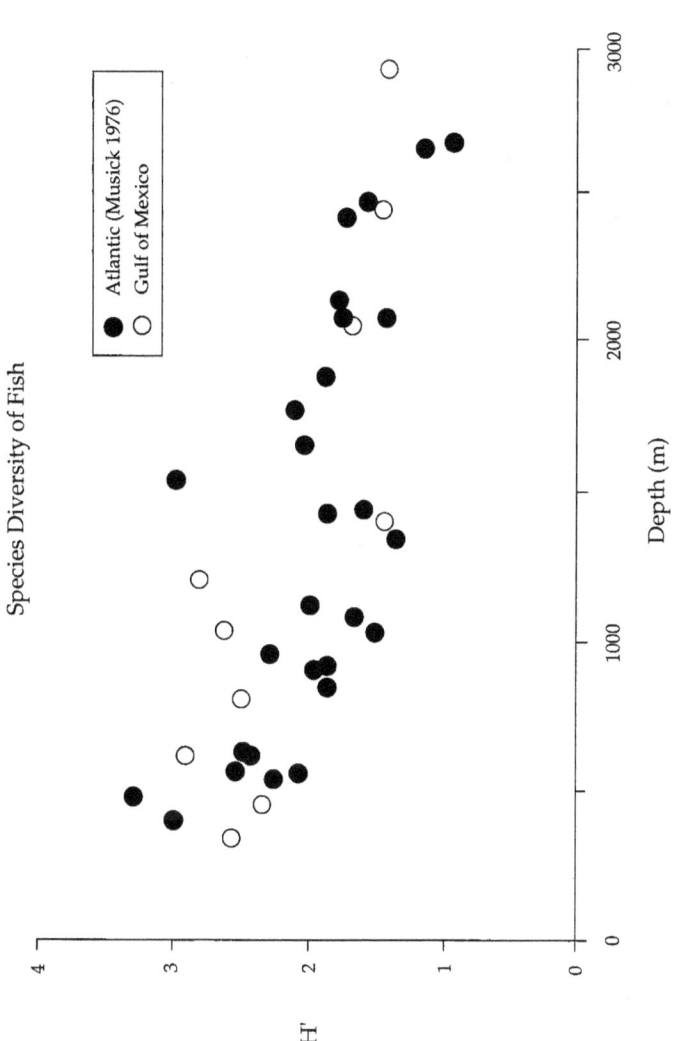

Figure 11. Comparision of fish diversity levels, by depth, between the Gulf of Mexico and the Atlantic (Musick 1976) continental slopes.

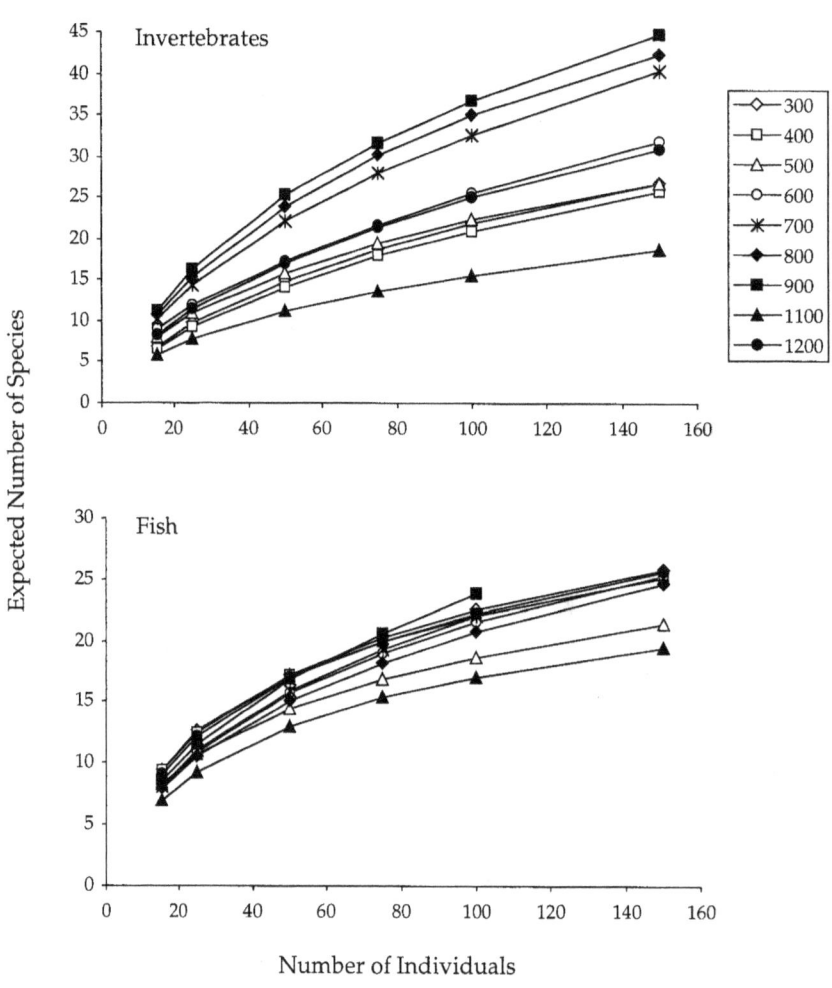

Figure 12. Results of rarefaction analyses for megafaunal fish and invertrebrate data by depth.

For the invertebrates, 465 (86%) of the total 538 taxa collected were represented by fewer than 60 specimens, but 22 taxa were represented by more than 300 specimens. However, among this group were four species that represent incidental species (e.g., small isopods and barnacles) contained in the tows. Although the numbers appear large, at least compared to the fish, even these data were not adequate to determine trends among regions, seasons, years, and depths. For the most part, a few large trawl catches comprise most of the data for each of the abundant species.

Nevertheless, some useful information was obtained from the megafauna collections. The complete data and detailed life history accounts can be found in Gallaway et al. (1988c). These data are synthesized below.

The length-weight data represent the largest of the life history data sets (Gallaway et al. 1988c). The relationships, even when pooled, all exhibited very tight fits to a linear regression, indicating low variability across seasons, years, and regions. These relationships can therefore be used as a predevelopment, baseline measure of megafaunal health or condition. The relationships also enable one to estimate biomass levels of megafauna given numbers and size distribution.

The length data showed ovigerous females of a number of invertebrates to have been significantly larger than males and non-ovigerous females—not a surprising result. Our data were not adequate to determine any seasonal or spatial patterns in the distribution of decapod crustaceans in a given reproductive state.

Although the size frequency data were often bi- or multimodal, indicating the possibility of multiple age groups, the sampling schedule was not frequent enough to delineate growth patterns. More frequent sampling at fixed locations than was planned for the NGOMCS Study would be required. The data suggest, however, that with adequate sampling (e.g., monthly) size groups or cohorts could be followed through time, yielding growth information.

We were able to obtain reasonably good trophic information from a limited number of specimens representing eight species of fish. Poor success in obtaining trophic information from fish raised from great depths is not unusual. Complete data for all fish, although fragmentary, is found in Gallaway et al. (1988c). Of the eight species, four were generally distributed at depths of about 500 m or less. Two (*Coelorinchus caribbaeus* and *Poecilopsetta beani*) fed mainly on polychaetes and amphipods, respectively. The other two (*Chloropthalmus agassizi* and *Bembrops gobiodes*) were predatory on larger forms, feeding mainly on fish and natantia, respectively.

Dibranchus atlanticus occurred over a wide depth range, but was most abundant at depths of 500 to 800 m. While the biomass data would indicate that this small predator fed largely on small hermit crabs (pagurids) and polychaetes, these data are misleading since pagurids actually occurred in only two of 33 stomachs. The primary food of this species consisted of amphipods and polychaetes. *Nezumia aequalis* had a depth distribution similar to *Dibranchus atlanticus* but fed almost exclusively on natantia (82%), based upon the contents of 13 stomachs.

Specimens of *Gadomus longifillis* and *Synaphobranchus oregoni* from which we were able to obtain stomachs in good condition were largely associated depths between 800 and 1,200 m The diet of *Synaphobranchus oregoni* consisted of fish and natantia, whereas *Gadomus longifillis* fed mainly on natantia and copepods.

The biochemistry work on the NGOMCS Study, conducted to compliment the food habits investigation, showed that the megafauna of the continental slope of the northern Gulf of Mexico reflect the signatures of planktonic as well as terrestrial biogenic and petroleum hydrocarbons. Biogenic hydrocarbons of planktonic origin were the most prevalent, especially in the eastern Gulf.

CONCLUSIONS

The results of our analysis of the data segregated by 100-m depth intervals provides little or no support for the hypothesis that there are three distinct and homogenous faunal bands on the upper slope between depths of 300 and 1,000 to 1,200 m. Macrofauna density, while highly variable between these depths, reflects no pronounced trend of decline (see Figure 6) and the polychaete density data by species reflect that while few species are restricted to the shallower depths and a few species occur at the deeper depths only, the vast majority occur throughout the depth range in question (see Table 3).

The megafaunal density data suggest two to three peaks in abundance at depths of roughly 300, 700, and 1,000 to 1,200 m (see Figures 9 and 10). However, when the data are examined on a species-by-species basis (e.g., Table 4), a continuum of overlapping distributions is seen grading from species restricted to shallower depths, to species generally restricted to mid-depths within the range in question, to species occurring at the deeper depths within the range. Sampling at broadly-spaced intervals within these distributions would suggest zonation whereas results of sampling at a less-coarse interval reflects a pattern of a non-repeating sequence of species aggregated along the depth gradient. We conclude that the existing data discount the idea that there are three distinct megafaunal assemblages represented between the shelf edge and 1,000 to 1,200 m and that, within each of these, the fauna is homogenous. The fauna clearly changes with depth as described above.

Based upon our observations, the continental slope fauna in the Gulf of Mexico appears to differ from the slope fauna in the U.S. Atlantic in several ways. First, Gulf meiofaunal densities appear to be higher than those reported for the Atlantic. In fact, the meiofaunal densities observed in this program are among the highest recorded in any deep-sea habitat. Gulf densities of macrofauna, however, were generally lower than densities observed in contemporary continental slope studies conducted in the Atlantic, especially at depths shallower than 1,000 m. In contrast, diversity of Gulf macrofauna at sites on the upper slope (<1,000 m) was observed to be much higher than was observed at depths less than 1,000 m on the Atlantic slope (see Fig. 8). The shallow Gulf slope was characterized by high diversity and low abundance as compared to the same region of the Atlantic slope.

As noted above, the faunal composition of the Gulf megafauna changes continually with depth such that a distinct upper slope fauna penetrates to about 1,200 m or so. A distinct deep-slope fauna appears present below 2,500 m. A broad transition zone characterized by low abundance and diversity occurs between depths of 1,200 m and 2,500 m. Fish diversity on the Gulf was observed to be high between 500 and 1,200 m, and then exhibited a step decline. Below 1,200 m, fish diversity was uniform at about one-half the level observed at shallower depths (see Fig. 11). This pattern contrasts greatly with that observed on the Atlantic slope. On the Atlantic slope, fish data reflected a near linear or exponential decay in diversity with depth.

The results of the NGOMCS study provide a snapshot of the Gulf slope environment and biota as it existed in the mid- to late 1980's. The findings of this study provide a point of reference for the recent MMS-sponsored deep-sea study being conducted by Texas A&M University. If the general observations described herein are repeated, then it will be clearly evident that the Gulf slope system differs from that of the Atlantic.

LITERATURE CITED

Brooks, J.M., M.C. Kennicutt II, R.R. Bidigare, and R.R. Fay. 1985. Hydrates, oil seepage and chemosynthetic ecosystems on the Gulf of Mexico slope. EOS. 66:105.

Carney, R.S., R.L. Haedrich, and G.T. Rowe. 1983. Zonation of fauna in the deep sea. Pages 371-398 in G.T. Rowe (ed.), Deep-Sea Biology. John Wiley & Sons, New York. 560 pp.

Carney, R.S. 2001. Management applicability of contemporary deep-sea ecology and re-evaluation of Gulf of Mexico studies. U.S. Dept. of the Interior, Minerals Management Service, New Orleans, LA. OCS Study MMS 2001-095. 170 pp.

Coull, B.C., R.L. Ellison, J.W. Fleeger, R.P. Higgins, W.D. Hope, W.D. Hummon, R.M. Rieger, W.E. Sterrer, H. Thiel, and J.H. Tietjen. 1977. Quantitative estimates of the meiofauna from the deep sea off North Carolina, U.S.A. Mar. Biol. 39:233-240.

Fauble, A. 1982. Determination of individual meiofauna dry weight values in relation to definite size classes. Cahierss de Biologie Marine, Tome XXIII:339-345.

Gallaway, B.J. (ed.). 1988a. Northern Gulf of Mexico Continental Slope Study, final report: Year 4. Volume I: Executive summary. U.S. Dept. of the Interior, Minerals Management Service, New Orleans, LA. OCS Study MMS 88-0052. 69 pp.

Gallaway, B.J. (ed.). 1988b. Northern Gulf of Mexico Continental Slope Study, final report: Year 4. Volume II: Synthesis report. U.S. Dept. of the Interior, Minerals Management Service, New Orleans, LA. OCS Study MMS 88-0053. 318 pp.

Gallaway, B.J. (ed.). 1988c. Northern Gulf of Mexico Continental Slope Study, final report: Year 4. Volume III: Appendices. U.S. Dept. of the Interior, Minerals Management Service, New Orleans, LA. OCS Study MMS 88-0054. 378 pp.

Gallaway, B.J. and M.C. Kennicutt II. 1988. Chapter 2: The characterization of benthic habitats of the northern Gulf of Mexico. Pages 2-1 to 2-45 *in* B.J. Gallaway (ed.). 1988. Northern Gulf of Mexico Continental Slope Study, final report: Year 4. Volume III: Appendices. U.S. Dept. of the Interior, Minerals Management Service, New Orleans, LA. OCS Study MMS 88-0054, 378 pp.

Gallaway, B.J., R.L. Howard, and G.F. Hubbard. 1988a. Chapter 3: Observations on the distribution and abundance of the meiofauna of the continental slope of the northern Gulf of Mexico. Pages 3-1 to 3-15 *in* B.J. Gallaway (ed.). 1988. Northern Gulf of Mexico Continental Slope Study, final report: Year 4. Volume III: Appendices. U.S. Dept. of the Interior, Minerals Management Service, New Orleans, LA. OCS Study MMS 88-0054. 378 pp.

Gallaway, B.J., R.L. Howard, and G.F. Hubbard. 1988b. Chapter 4: The macrofauna of the continental slope of the northern Gulf of Mexico: community structure, diversity and abundance as compared to environmental features. Pages 4-1 to 4-70 *in* B.J. Gallaway (ed.). 1988. Northern Gulf of Mexico Continental Slope Study, final report: Year 4. Volume III: Appendices. U.S. Dept. of the Interior, Minerals Management Service, New Orleans, LA. OCS Study MMS 88-0054. 378 pp.

Gallaway, B.J., L.R. Martin and R.L. Howard (eds.). 1988c. Northern Gulf of Mexico Continental Slope Study, annual report: Year 3. Volume II: Technical Narrative. U.S. Dept. of the Interior, Minerals Management Service, New Orleans, LA. OCS Study MMS 88-060. 586 pp.

Hubbard, G.F., R.L. Howard, and B.J. Gallaway. 1988. Loricifera, a recently described phylum occurring in the northern Gulf of Mexico. Northeast Gulf Science 10(1):49-50.

Hurlbert, S.H. 1971. The nonconcept of species diversity: A critique and alternative parameters. Ecology. 52:577-586.

Kennicutt, M.C. II, J.L. Sericano, T.L. Wade, F. Alcazar, and J.M. Books. 1987. High molecular weight hydrocarbons in Gulf of Mexico continental slope sediments. Deep-Sea Res. 34(3):403-424.

Kristensen, R.M. 1983. Loricifera, a new phylum with aschelminthes characters from the meiobenthos. Zeitung für Zoologische Systematik und Evolutionsforschung 21:163-180.

Lacerda, C.P., M.C. Kennicutt II, and J.M. Brooks. 1987. The distribution of dibenzothiophens in the Gulf of Mexico sediments. Applied Geochemistry. 2(3):297-304.

Maciolek-Blake, N., P.D. Boehm, B. Hecker, J.F. Grassle, D. McGrath, A.G. Requejo, B. Brown, C.M. Cetta, D. Dade, S. Freitas, and R. Petrecca. 1985. Study of biological processes on the U.S. mid-Atlantic slope and rise: First interim report. Prepared for U.S. Dept. of the Interior, Minerals Management Service. 99 pp. + appendices.

Maciolek, N., B. Hecker, C.A. Butman, J.F. Grassle, W.B. Dade, P.D. Boehm, W.G. Steinhauer, V. Starczk, E. Baptiste, R.E. Ruff, and B. Brown. 1986. Study of biological processes on the U.S. North Atlantic slope and rise. U.S. Dept. of the Interior, Minerals Management Service. MMS 86-0022. 201 pp. + appendices.

Musick, J.J. 1976. Community structure of fishes on the continental slope and rise off the middle Atlantic Coast. U.S. Joint Oceanographic Assembly, Edinburgh.

Pequegnat, W.E. 1983. The ecological communities of the continental slope and adjacent regimes of the northern Gulf of Mexico. Report to the U.S. Dept. of the Interior, Minerals Management Service, Metairie, LA, by TerEco Corporation, College Station, TX. 398 pp. + appendices.

Pequegnat, W.E., B.J. Gallaway, and L.H. Pequegnat. 1990. Aspects of the ecology of the deepwater fauna of the Gulf of Mexico. American Zoologist 30: 45-64.

Rowe, G.T. 1971. Benthic biomass and surface productivity. Pages 441-454 *in* J.D. Costlow, Jr. (ed.). Fertility of the Sea, Vol. 2. Gordon and Breach, New York.

Rowe, G.T., P.T. Polloni, and S.G. Horner. 1974. Benthic biomass estimates from the northwestern Atlantic Ocean and the northern Gulf of Mexico. Deep-Sea Res. 21:641-650.

Sanders, H.L. 1968. Marine benthic diversity: A comparative study. Amer. Nat. 102:243-282.

Smith, W.L. and J.F. Grassle. 1977. Sampling properties of a family of diversity measures. Biometrics. 33:283-291.

Thiel, H. 1983. Meiobenthos and nanobenthos of the deep sea. Pages 167-230 *in* G.T. Rowe (ed.). Deep-Sea Biology, Chapter 5. John Wiley & Sons, New York. 560 pp.

Tietjen, J.H. 1971. Ecology and distribution of deep-sea meiobenthos off North Carolina. Deep-Sea Res. 18:941-954.

Wigley, R.L. and A.D. McIntyre. 1964. Some quantitative comparisons of offshore meiobenthos and macrobenthos south of Martha's Vineyard. Limnol. Oceanogr. 9:485-493.

APPENDIX 1

SUMMARY OF TRAWLING EFFORT

APPENDIX 1. SUMMARY OF TRAWLING EFFORT

CRUISE I - MMS-NGOMCS TRAWL STATIONS, NOVEMBER 1983

Station	Depth (m)	On-Bottom Position N. Lat (Deg.).	On-Bottom Position W. Long. (Deg.)	Duration (Hrs:Min)	Remarks	QA
C-1	329	28.044	90.175	1:09	5 containers (2 fish, 3 invertebrates)	(1)
C-2	786	27.533	90.053	1:14	All fish (except ophidiids) kept for HC	(1)
C-3	850	27.480	90.033	2:30	3 buckets and 3 jars	(1)
C-4	1440	27.254	89.476	1:21	Small catch (trawl bridge twisted)	(2)
C-5	2400	26.565	89.332	5:19	Trawl malfunctioned, minimal catch	(2)

[1]Quantitative

[2]Non-quantitative

CRUISE II - MMS-NGOMCS TRAWL STATIONS, 7-19 APRIL 1984

Station	Depth (m)	On-Bottom Position N. Lat (Deg.).	On-Bottom Position W. Long. (Deg.)	Duration (Hrs:Min)	Remarks	QA
W-1	342	27.370	93.336	1:08	5 gal. shell hash (dead clams) plus 1 bucket, 1 jar	(1)
W-2	576-732	27.245	93.189	1:02	1 bucket, 1 jar	(1)
W-3	792-864	27.084	93.236	2:39	3 containers	(1)
W-4	1372-1454	26.444	93.186	2:18	Palm fronds and sargassum (1 bucket of specimens	(1)
W-5	2322-2305	26.171	93.246	2:37	Port side door had turned over 1 complete revolution. Both doors covered with traces of mud. 2 containers: 1 vial and 1 9-oz jar	(2)
C-1	329-347	28.033	90.150	1:05	2 buckets and 1 16-0z jar	(1)
C-2	603	27.544	90.060	1:04	Many brittle stars (1 bucket and 1 gal. jar)	(1)
C-3	805	27.497	90.067	2:19	1 container	(1)
C-4	1358-1518	27.281	89.436	2:00	2 1-gal jars	(1)
C-5	2412-2390	27.014	89.303	2:16	Poor catch (1 gal. jar)	(1)
E-1	375-358	28.265	86.031	1:17	Good catch	(1)
E-2	603-640	28.176	86.148	0:59	Lazy line wrapped around cod end. 1 bucket	(2)
E-3	840	28.107	86.256	2:14	2 buckets	(1)
E-4	1170	28.060	86.353	2:07	3 buckets	(1)
E-5	2881-2834	28.019	86.401	2:12	Poor trawl--doors probably collapsed	(2)

[1]Quantitative

[2]Non-quantitative

CRUISE III - MMS-NGOMCS TRAWL STATIONS, NOVEMBER-DECEMBER 1984

Station	Depth (m)	On-Bottom Position		Duration (Hrs:Min)	Remarks	QA
		N. Lat (Deg.).	W. Long. (Deg.)			
C-1	366-326	28.023	90.148	1:03	No problems noted	(1)
C-2	632	27.543	90.075	1:23	Counted and discarded 718 ophiuroids. 3 buckets (2 fish, 1 invertebrate)	(1)
C-3	841-764	27.489	90.078	1:09	Fair trawl (sample in 3 buckets)	(1)
C-4	1420-1600	27.277	89.455	2:00	Not many animals (low biomass). Lot of bottom debris (burnt coal-type material). 1 5-gal. Bucket	(2)
C-5	2486-2523	26.567	89.306	2:03	Good haul	(1)
C-6	501-448	28.01	90.051	1:00	No problems noted	(1)
C-7	896-1033	27.445	90.015	1:02	Due to sudden rise in bottom stopped wire out at 3289 m and turned vessel to 045 deg. At 1001 hrs. turned to 090 deg. as bottom still rising (outside acceptable range)	(2)
C-8	1064	27.311	89.489	1:34	Greatest variety so far; baby giant squid, pteropods, shrimp, fish, benthosaurus	(1)
C-9	1309-1317	27.295	89.479	0:50	Large mud ball. Trawl anchored vessel	(2)
C-10	1680-1790	27.25	89.422	2:02	Lots of mud--2.5 tons. Not much biota-- probably some lost with mud lumps (clays)	(2)
C-11	2085-2063	27.137	89.368	2:00	Lots of trash--terrigenous material, sar- gassum, rocks, starfish. 1 5-gal bucket	(2)
C-12	-	-	-	-	Gear problems, no trawl	(2)

[1]Quantitative

[2]Non-quantitative

CRUISE IV - MMS-NGOMCS TRAWL STATIONS, MAY 1985

Station	Depth (m)	On-Bottom Position N. Lat (Deg.).	W. Long. (Deg.)	Duration (Hrs:Min)	Remarks	QA
E-1	351-357	28.448	86.042	1:00	4 buckets, good tow	(1)
E-1a	351-351	28.906	86.407	0:55	3 buckets, good tow	(1)
E-1b	346-344	28.311	85.739	0:58	2 buckets plus 1 gallon	(1)
E-1c	353-347	28.219	85.566	0:58	High shrimp catch, many fish	(1)
E-2	613-618	28.268	86.201	1:00	Good catches	(1)
E-2a	625-625	28.584	86.762	1:35	7 buckets + 2 gal. Containers	(1)
E-2b	625-600	28.316	86.316	0:59	4 buckets	(1)
E-2c	620-616	28.226	86.111	0:59	No problems noted	(1)
E-2d	624-631	28.127	85.860	1:00	7 buckets, rocks and wood	(1)
E-2e	629-629	28.018	85.661	1:00	2 buckets, no problems	(1)
E-3	871-871	28.160	86.399	1:00	1 bucket, no problems	(1)
E-3a	841-783	28.499	86.969	0:44	4 buckets	(1)
E-3b	845-823	28.119	86.286	1:00	3 buckets	(1)
E-3c	838-847	28.267	86.604	1:07	No problems noted	(1)
E-3d	845-856	28.373	86.808	1:01	No problems noted	(1)
E-5	-	-		-	Gear problems, no trawl	(2)
WC-5	402-444	27.784	91.729	1:00	No problems noted	(1)
WC-8	486-472	27.862	90.764	1:04	6 buckets	(1)
WC-9	807-695	27.713	91.255	0:59	4 buckets	(1)

[1] Quantitative
[2] Non-quantitative

CRUISE V - MMS-NGOMCS TRAWL STATIONS, JUNE 1985

Station	Depth (m)	On-Bottom Position		Duration (Hrs:Min)	Remarks	QA
		N. Lat (Deg.).	W. Long. (Deg.)			
WC-1	344-393	27.716	92.868	0:45	Net clogged with sargassum, not on bottom long, irregular bottom	(2)
WC-2	518-585	27.752	92.483	1:00	2 buckets	(1)
WC-3	781-768	27.587	92.378	0:59	Bridle twisted nearly to doors, doors only open to 3 m on retrieval	(2)
WC-4	527-516	27.719	92.154	0:58	2 buckets	(1)
WC-6	543-783	27.712	91.549	1:06	12 buckets, coral reef fauna	(1)
WC-7	457-472	27.759	91.227	1:00	Noted as rope & worm station, strong current	(1)
WC-10	741-752	27.755	90.800	1:00	Tow too fast; not enough scope, meager catch	(2)
WC-11	1247-1024	27.412	92.634	1:00	4 buckets	(1)
WC-12	1236-1170	27.327	91.522	1:00	No problems noted	(1)

[1]Quantitative

[2]Non-quantitative

The Department of the Interior Mission

As the Nation's principal conservation agency, the Department of the Interior has responsibility for most of our nationally owned public lands and natural resources. This includes fostering sound use of our land and water resources; protecting our fish, wildlife, and biological diversity; preserving the environmental and cultural values of our national parks and historical places; and providing for the enjoyment of life through outdoor recreation. The Department assesses our energy and mineral resources and works to ensure that their development is in the best interests of all our people by encouraging stewardship and citizen participation in their care. The Department also has a major responsibility for American Indian reservation communities and for people who live in island territories under U.S. administration.

The Minerals Management Service Mission

As a bureau of the Department of the Interior, the Minerals Management Service's (MMS) primary responsibilities are to manage the mineral resources located on the Nation's Outer Continental Shelf (OCS), collect revenue from the Federal OCS and onshore Federal and Indian lands, and distribute those revenues.

Moreover, in working to meet its responsibilities, the **Offshore Minerals Management Program** administers the OCS competitive leasing program and oversees the safe and environmentally sound exploration and production of our Nation's offshore natural gas, oil and other mineral resources. The MMS **Minerals Revenue Management** meets its responsibilities by ensuring the efficient, timely and accurate collection and disbursement of revenue from mineral leasing and production due to Indian tribes and allottees, States and the U.S. Treasury.

The MMS strives to fulfill its responsibilities through the general guiding principles of: (1) being responsive to the public's concerns and interests by maintaining a dialogue with all potentially affected parties and (2) carrying out its programs with an emphasis on working to enhance the quality of life for all Americans by lending MMS assistance and expertise to economic development and environmental protection.